Three-Dimensional Papercraft

Dedicated to
Samuel, Sasha, Jaya and Matthew.
With all my love.

Three-Dimensional Papercraft

Dawn Allen

SEARCH PRESS

First published in Great Britain 2007

Search Press Limited
Wellwood, North Farm Road,
Tunbridge Wells, Kent TN2 3DR

Text copyright © Dawn Allen 2007

Photographs by Storm Photographic Studios, except for step-by-step photographs on pages 12–20, 24–32, 36–42, 46–51, 54–58, 62–65 and 68–74, which were shot at Roddy Paine Photographic Studios.

Photographs and design copyright © Search Press Ltd 2007

ISBN-10: 1-84448-219-7
ISBN-13: 978-1-84448-219-1

The Publishers and author can accept no responsibility for any consequences arising from the information, advice or instructions given in this publication.

Readers are permitted to reproduce any of the items in this book for their personal use, or for the purposes of selling for charity, free of charge and without the prior permission of the Publishers. Any use of the items for commercial purposes is not permitted without the prior permission of the Publishers.

Suppliers
If you have difficulty in obtaining any of the materials and equipment mentioned in this book, then please visit the Search Press website for details of suppliers:
www.searchpress.com

Publisher's note

All the step-by-step photographs in this book feature the author, Dawn Allen, demonstrating three-dimensional Papercraft. No models have been used.

Cover: A Rainbow of Colours
This three-dimensional picture clearly illustrates the depth that can be achieved with the correct shaping. The curve of the buds is clearly visible, as is the height between the layers and the fine cutting of the stems.

Acknowledgements

A very special thank-you to Ron, who has advised, supported and encouraged me in so many ways.

Many thanks to John Don of Personal Impressions for arranging and supplying all the stamping equipment, to Robin Sudbury at Absolutely Art for his help and assistance in selecting just the right prints, and to the Directors at John Arnold for all their help on the *Wildlife* series and *All Our Yesterdays* series.

I would like also to mention the assistance received from the British Museum in London.

I could not have achieved this book without the support of all these people and those at Search Press for all their hard work.

Thank you everyone.

Inca Stamps manufactured and supplied by Personal Impressions:
Rose Fairy (3023I); Iris Fairy (3017I); Nasturtium Fairy (3036P); Lilac Fairy (3025I); Red Clover Fairy (3024I).

Prints used from Absolutely Art:
Cherry Blossom Small (Manor Art 4221); Cherry Blossom Large (Manor Art 4222); Clematis (RS501–7004); Hibiscus (RS504–7079); Chef (RS501–7022); Golfer (RS502–7032); Fisherman (RS501–7033); Cricketer (RS501–7031); Judge (RS501–7020). Prints by Reina are copyrighted to Reina NY, all rights reserved.

Prints used from John Arnold:
African Wildlife: Lion (A); Leopard (B); Tiger (C); Cheetah (D).
Temptations: B. *Bygone Days*: 1, 2 and 3.

Page 1: Masque
The dark blue velvet set against the gold creates a dramatic backdrop for this masque sticker and illustrates the impact that can be made with the use of colours.

Page 2: Cherry Blossom
A plain snow-white background captures the beauty and innocence of this delicate blossom perfectly.

Page 3: Iris Fairy
Peeking through the flowers, this Iris Fairy makes a stunning card. The lightness of the picture contrasts well against the deep green backing card, while the delicate flower-patterned parchment paper creates an enchantingly delicate effect.

Opposite: *Detail from* You're Late
This close-up of the two characters shows how important it is to get the slope of the floor correct to enable feet to be in the correct position, and also shows how shadows help to create the three-dimensional effect.

Contents

Introduction

Three-dimensional decoupage is the craft of cutting, shaping and layering paper to create a three-dimensional image. The origins of the craft lie in the late 18th century when Mary Delany began making paper collages, or 'mosaicks' as she called them. She was renowned for having an eye for botanical detail and would cut minute pieces of coloured paper and stick them on to a black background to represent each part of a specimen. She created over a thousand collages in this manner and some of her work can be seen at the British Museum in London.

While the craft has progressed a great deal since then, it is fair to say that much of the original concept still remains. In the mid- to late-20th century it developed into a three-dimensional art form with cut pieces from several identical prints being layered on to a base image. Subsequently this wonderful craft has been adapted, refined and made readily available to everyone.

You can create three-dimensional pictures from almost any type of printed image. Printed sheets for cards and pictures are widely available but you can make your own from art stamps, outline stickers and so forth and these can then be hand-coloured. Cards can also be enhanced with embellishments such as feathers, buttons, ribbons and similar items.

Throughout this book I show some of the skills and techniques required to create a successful picture. The projects have been chosen to give you an idea of the type of pictures and cards that can be created by using the various different cutting, shaping and gluing techniques.

I do hope you find this book interesting and helpful. Remember that it is your work: you can not make a mistake – it will just be a little different. I wish you every success and I hope you gain as much pleasure from this craft as I have.

Materials

To make a three-dimensional picture, several identical prints are required. Prints that are suitable for pictures and cards are widely available in many different designs and sizes.

Cards and pictures are made in the same way, except that fewer prints are required for cards because less detail is needed. On average, six or seven prints will make a good picture, and four or five will make a good card.

Cards and papers

There are a large number of ready-made card blanks available in various colours and designs. It is important to choose the right colour card blank to complement the image. Blanks are available with fancy edges and with or without apertures. Alternatively, you can cut your own card to size from individual sheets of card using a paper trimmer or a metal ruler and a craft knife.

There is an extensive range of fantastic papers and envelopes in various weights and sizes. Glittered, textured, holographic, parchment and lovely handmade papers are all now widely available. These papers can be used for mat mounting (layering different coloured cards or paper on to a backing card to create a backdrop), covering a card, or to create an insert. Never discard unused pieces of paper or card, as even the smallest scrap can be useful as a backing piece, or for use with a craft punch to create a decoration for your cards.

The paper used is very important: if it is of poor quality it will flake when it is cut, and if you are using glaze, it will need more than one coat as it will be absorbed by the paper. High-gloss papers like photographic paper should be avoided as they can wrinkle when shaped.

Printed sheets

Pictures are usually made from prints. These can be obtained in packs which contain sufficient sheets to complete the task. You can also buy prints individually but make sure that you buy a sufficient quantity – it is important to have enough prints to complete your picture. The more prints you use, the more detailed the finished picture will be.

There are two different types of printed sheets for cutting and making three-dimensional cards. Firstly, there are sheets with four or more identical images from which you can select the parts to create your own interpretation of the three-dimensional effect.

Secondly, there are step-by-step sheets available. These are printed sheets on which parts of the picture are numbered in the order in which they are to be cut and used.

Outline stickers

Three or four outline stickers of the same design can be placed on to a white card. These can then be coloured and used to create a three-dimensional image.

Rubber stamps

This is a design or image made on a rubber base, which is then mounted on to a block of wood. When the stamp is inked it can be printed on to paper or card four or five times. The print can then be coloured with a colouring medium of your choice and used to make a card or picture.

Embellishments

There is an extensive range of embellishments available to decorate your finished work. Cards in particular look fantastic when decorated with ribbons, beads, eyelets, feathers, buttons, motifs or simply a greeting such as 'happy birthday' or 'congratulations'. The choice is endless.

Craft punches are very popular as they last forever and you can punch a design from any odd scrap of paper or card so that nothing is wasted. Try to use colours, styles and textures that complement each other to create a harmonious look.

Pictures do not usually require additional embellishments, but a subtle addition (such as a butterfly added to a flower) can give the picture that little bit extra. Bear in mind that over-embellishing your work can detract from the finished piece.

Other materials

Craft knife and blades There are many different types of craft knives available. Select one that is comfortable to hold and will accept a 10A scalpel blade. The knife I use throughout this book is a lightweight plastic one with a retractable blade. Knives with snap-off blades are not suitable because the blades are too thick and inflexible. As a general rule one blade should be sufficient to completely cut one small picture. If the blade is blunt the cut will not be smooth and sharp. Always dispose of old blades safely in a secure container.

Cutting mat Always cut on a cutting mat or thick card: wooden or other hard surfaces will blunt your blade. The best thing to use is a self-healing cutting mat. This seals itself after a fine cut and it therefore retains a smooth and flat cutting surface.

Scissors My long-handled scissors are 11½cm (4½in) long and have straight-pointed blades that are 2½cm (1in) long.

Shaping tools I prefer to use shaping tools made from wood because plastic or metal tools can easily mark the paper. The tools are variously shaped and are used for different purposes.

Eraser or foam pad These will provide a soft base on which to shape pieces with your shaping tools. A make up pad is ideal.

Silicone sealant This is thick silicone-based glue that dries hard, and is used to create space between layers.

Three-dimensional foam squares These are small double-sided adhesive squares filled with foam. They come in different sizes and depths.

Tweezers Long straight tweezers approximately 17cm (6¾in) are ideal to use with large cut pieces, and angled tweezers approximately 15cm (6in) long are better for holding and placing the smaller pieces.

Cocktail sticks These are used to position pieces more precisely once they are placed.

Palette You can use any non-absorbent surface as a palette to mix paints or inks. I use a sheet of acetate.

Paper glaze and brush cleaner Glaze is a paper varnish that when applied smoothly to the finished picture will create the effect of fine porcelain and will also enhance the colours. Use a cleaner that is recommended for use with your glaze.

Paintbrush A brush that will not moult is essential and I have found a size 2 camel hair brush works well for glazing and painting.

Paper guillotine This allows you to cut perfectly straight edges.

Ruler This helps you to fold and crease card.

Waterbased glue This is a clear adhesive glue that dries almost on contact. Use it sparingly.

Double-sided tape Both sides of this tape are covered in adhesive, protected by a peel-off backing strip. It will stick two surfaces together securely.

Adhesive dots These are supplied in a container which dispenses a row of adhesive dots that allow two surfaces to be joined together.

Low-tack tape This has a mild adhesive so that pieces attached with this can be relocated without marking the paper. It can be used on all types of card and paper, including parchment paper, but does not create a permanent bond.

Stamping mat This is a foam mat that helps to create a clear sharp image whilst stamping.

Craft scissors or rotary paper trimmer These are useful for adding fancy edges to cards. The scissors allow different shapes, but a rotary paper trimmer is easier to use for straight lines.

Double-ended felt tip pens These pens have a one thick and one fine end, making them very useful for both general and detail colouring.

Techniques

In this section I explain how to use the equipment to achieve great results every time. Before you start cutting the prints, it will be necessary to formulate a plan in your mind of the pieces needed to make a three-dimensional picture. One picture will act as the base from which the three-dimensional image will be built up in layers using pieces from the other prints.

Please bear in mind that the amount of detail you can achieve will depend on the number of prints you use. As a general rule the more prints you use, the greater the detail.

Cutting with a craft knife

The technique for cutting with a craft knife is very simple but it takes practice. By cutting into the paper at an angle you are effectively bevelling the paper by cutting away the underneath part. This means that the white edge of the paper will not be visible.

Keep your touch light: you do not have to press hard if the blade is sharp (a blunt blade will give jagged edges and can tear the paper). Imagine that the knife is a pencil and you are drawing an outline around the piece you are cutting. It is that easy – just remember to cut on a cutting mat, or thick card.

Tip
If you are left-handed, cut around the shape in an anticlockwise direction.

1. Hold the knife at a slight angle, as you would hold a pen or a pencil. An angle of twenty-five to thirty degrees from the horizontal is both ideal and comfortable.

2. Cut curves in a clockwise direction, moving your whole arm, not just your wrist. Keep the movement steady and flowing around the curve, working in a clockwise direction.

3. Make sure that you keep the blade at the correct angle for cutting straight lines.

4. Move your whole arm, not just your wrist, to ensure the movement is steady and straight.

Tip
Try to relax: the more relaxed you are, the easier you will find it to cut.

Cutting with scissors

There are disadvantages to using scissors instead of a craft knife because it is difficult to get them into small spaces as precisely as a craft knife and it is not so easy to get a bevelled edge. This means that you may end up with white edges showing. If so, it will be necessary to colour the edges using coloured pens or pencils a shade lighter than the actual image.

1. Hold the scissors at a slight angle, and support them with your hand. This will steady you as you cut.

2. Cut into the piece to ensure that you do not get a white line on the outside edge of the piece.

3. Continue cutting until the shape is completely cut out.

Overcutting

When an object overlaps another (such as a petal over a leaf), it is necessary to cut away part of the petal whilst cutting out the leaf shape. This ensures that when you cut the exact shape of the petal from another print and place it over the leaf, no hole is seen behind the petal.

1. Begin cutting the background shape (in this example, the leaf) as normal.

2. Continue cutting through any shapes in the foreground (in this example, the flower) where the background shape would lie.

3. Continue cutting until the background shape is completely cut out.

Cutting fine detail

Furring and feathering

Cutting grass, hair, feathers or fur is not difficult, and is called furring or feathering. You can use either a knife or scissors but you will always get a finer finish with a knife. The 'secret' lies in the way the knife or scissors are angled. Do make sure that you are cutting with the lie of the hair or the animal will look either in need of some grooming or very scared!

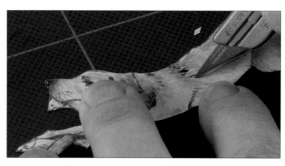

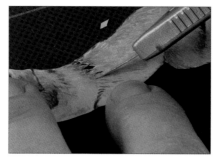

1. Identify the area to be furred or feathered. Cut into the fur with very short movements.

2. Turn the knife through ninety degrees as shown and cut in the alternate direction.

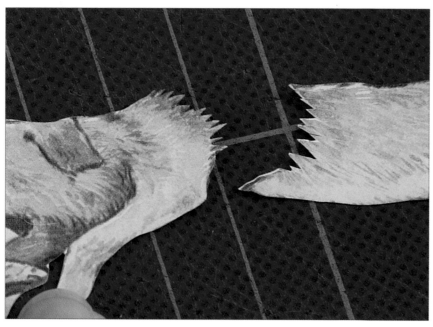

3. Continue until the area is completed.

Tip

With this type of cutting it is sometimes necessary to colour in the edges. Do this using pens or pencils. Always use a shade lighter than the actual image and if you colour in between the cuts where white edges show, do it on the reverse side so that you do not accidentally mark your picture.

Fine lines

When cutting very fine lines such as twigs, stems and washing lines, do not cut too close to the edge of the piece. Cut with only a slight bevel. Do not attempt to colour in this fine edge, as this will only serve to highlight the thickness of the piece.

1. Hold the knife at about five degrees from the horizontal. This makes you less likely to cut though the piece. Leave some white space at the side of the line.

2. If possible, cut the fine line in one smooth movement. It does not matter if you cut some of the background in, as when the piece is mounted you will not see it. In fact, overcutting will create an 'anchoring point' when assembling the picture.

> **Tip**
>
> For rigging on boats, it is possible to use fine cotton thread. This can be strengthened by coating it in a quick-drying clear glue. Leave the cotton to dry completely before use: this will give it strength without thickness.

3. Turn the work round and repeat on the other side of the line.

Rescuing a mistake

If you should cut thorough a piece by accident, do not panic.

1. Place the two broken pieces, face up, on to a white sticky label.

2. Use a craft knife to cut away the excess label. If the two ends do not join neatly, lightly colour the join on the front of the piece with a coloured pencil. No one will notice the join!

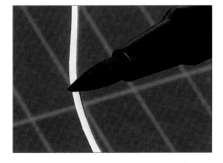

3. Use a felt-tip pen or pencil in a shade lighter than the actual image to colour in the edge where the label has been used. Do this on the reverse side, so that you do not acccidentally mark your picture.

Shaping

Shaping is an essential step in three-dimensional decoupage. You need to visualise the subject in real life and then re-create it in layers to give the picture a three-dimensional look. This may seem quite difficult to begin with but as with most things it comes easily with practice.

It is necessary to use a pencil eraser or a foam pad as a base on which to shape the pieces. This creates a soft but supportive surface under the paper which allows the piece to adapt to the required shape or curvature.

Shaping is usually done on the blank side of the piece. If you do not like the shape you have made you can roll it out by turning it over and shape in the opposite direction. You can then start again without damaging the piece. This can be repeated until you have the desired effect.

Faces

A shaping tool with a spoon-shaped end, used in conjunction with an eraser, is ideal for shaping faces. The fine pointed end can be used for eyes if you wish to give them particular emphasis.

> # Tip
> Always hold the piece in position with tweezers to make sure it is correct before applying the mounting medium.

1. Place the piece face down on an eraser.

2. Work round the edges of the piece with the spoon-shaped end of the shaping tool.

3. The finished piece will have a slight curve to it which will add to the overall look of the finished piece of decoupage.

Leaves and petals

Depending on the shape you would like your petal to be, use either the spoon-shaped end or the barrel of the shaping tool as a roller in conjunction with the foam pad. Experiment with the different ends to get the best effect. Use the round-ended shaping tool for berries, placing the piece face down on the foam pad or eraser.

1. Place the piece face down on the foam pad.

2. Roll the barrel of the shaping tool across the piece.

3. The finished piece.

Scoring for boxes

Use the shaping tool with a pointed end for scoring along straight lines such as buildings and so forth. Score on the printed side of the work using a ruler in conjunction with the pointed end tool. This can be done on a normal cutting mat. Depending on the direction of the fold, you can use the chisel-ended tool to fold into the required shape.

1. Place the piece face up, and use a ruler to score a straight line with the pointed end of the shaping tool.

2. Turn the piece over, place the chisel-ended tip of the shaping tool on the score line, and use your finger to fold it into the required shape.

3. This technique is great for sharp, precise lines.

and gluing

...to use for creating the space between layers is silicone ... holds securely and dries very hard. Once dry, it will not ...nsuring the layers do not get flattened. Because of its ...y to obtain varying thicknesses between the layers of a picture. Applied with a cocktail stick, it is easier to control the amount required and allows maximum flexibility when positioning.

Another advantage of using silicone sealant is that once you have placed the piece on to your work it can be manoeuvred, tilted and even remounted as it takes some time for the silicone sealant to dry completely.

The other method of mounting the pieces is using foam squares. When using foam squares it can be difficult to obtain the right height and depth, and once the work is mounted on these it cannot easily be removed.

Ideally it is best to use curved or straight tweezers when mounting pieces. This will ensure that the works stays clean and free from unwanted marks and it is easier to see exactly where the piece needs to be placed.

A common question from beginners is 'how much depth should there be between layers?' In short, each picture will be individual, but as a general rule 3–5mm (¼in) between the base and first layer and approximately 2–3mm (⅛in) between subsequent layers. This will of course vary considerably between different subjects within the picture.

Silicone sealant

After trying many different methods, I have found that the easiest and cleanest way to apply dabs of silicone to the cut pieces is with a cocktail stick as shown in the following steps.

The cocktail stick should be cleaned after every application, so keep a clean piece of kitchen paper to hand to wipe it clean. If your cocktail stick is not clean the silicone will not roll off it easily or neatly.

Tip

If you smudge silicone on to your work, do not panic. Do not try to rub it off as it will leave a smear mark. Instead, allow it to dry and you will find it can be removed easily.

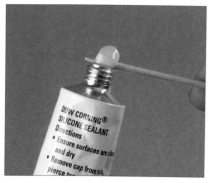

1. Apply silicone sealant on to the end of a cocktail stick.

2. Roll the silicone sealant on to the back of the piece. Larger pieces may need more than one dab of silicone (inset).

3. Pick the piece up with fine tweezers and place it on top of the picture.

Foam squares

The backing on these little squares can be very difficult to remove, particularly if you have short nails. The easiest way is to use the edge of a craft knife as shown.

1. Peel the foam squares off the sheet and place them individually on the back of the piece.

2. Use the blade of the scalpel to lift off the backing.

3. More foam squares can be placed on top of the first set, to lift the piece higher.

Tip

Do not use glue under finely-cut lines such as stems and stalks. These are light enough that they do not need any support, and glue will just make them look ugly.

4. Once the backing is removed, the piece can be placed with your fine tweezers.

Glazing

Glazing can be used to create a shiny effect and to give areas of colour more impact. I prefer to glaze only small parts of a picture, such as berries, the eyes of animals and other reflective objects. What to glaze is a matter of personal choice and is best left to the reader to decide.

It is only necessary to varnish the top layer of a picture, since this is the only part you will see when the picture is finished. When glazing finely cut pieces such as flower stems, carefully place a piece of card behind the stem to protect the base picture and remove the card when you have finished.

Do not attempt to glaze any work until the glue or silicone sealant is completely dry: I would recommend leaving your work for at least twelve hours. Always use a good brush so the hairs will not fall out on to the picture – a size 2 camel hair paintbrush works really well. Always clean your brush immediately after use, using a cleaner recommended for the type of glaze you are using.

The type of glaze must be suitable for use on paper, so test it on a scrap piece of the picture to make sure that the colour does not run before starting on the picture itself. Depending on the varnish used and the absorbency of the paper it may be necessary to apply two coats of glaze. If this is the case, the first coat should be left for at least twenty-four hours before applying the second one.

Glazing

Always store glaze in an upright position out of direct sunlight. If you should get an air bubble on your glazed piece, do not try and brush it out. Instead, use a pin to burst the air bubble.

> ## Tip
> There are waterbased glazes on the market but these tend to curl the paper if it is too thin. Once glaze is applied, it cannot be removed, so always test on a piece of scrap paper beforehand if you are not sure. If you are in any doubt, do not glaze.

> ## Safety note
> Always be careful when using glaze. Use it only in a well-ventilated area and avoid breathing in the fumes. Keep the glaze well away from naked flames. Children should not be allowed to use an oil-based glaze unsupervised.

1. Once you have finished your piece, leave it to dry for twenty-four hours. Use pieces of scrap paper to protect the area around the piece being glazed.

2. Load a camel hair brush with the glaze and allow the glaze to drop on to the top of the piece, then draw the glaze down the piece with the tip of the paintbrush.

3. Leave the glaze to dry completely, then remove the scrap paper.

The light blue oval mount with the dark blue background adds extra dimension to this relaxing picture.

o any picture is very important and different completely and dramatically alter the overall effect. y light, a darker background will give an impression of depth and will highlight the image itself. Experiment with different textures and colours until you find one you are happy with.

Try to select a background that complements and does not dominate the picture. Backgrounds with very bold patterns can be overpowering and detract from the three-dimensional effect.

If the picture is going to be framed I would advise against adding embellishments as it will make framing difficult. However, if you are creating a card rather than a picture then embellishments can work really well – with the correct selection, the design will be enhanced.

Choosing a background

Here I have shown several different backgrounds with the cherry blossom (below) placed on them to demonstrate the difference a background can make to a finished piece. We all have different tastes and ideas of what looks nice, so experiment until you find a background that you feel sets off your work to the best effect.

This picture of a cherry blossom was made up in a similar way to the project on pages 24–33, and would make an excellent greeting card for someone very special.

This picture, complete with the original background, is taped on to a picture mount ready for framing.

I have cut away the original background before mounting this on to a card which is covered in a pale pink parchment paper. A red eyelet has been inserted in each corner and a dark maroon ribbon threaded through the holes at the top and bottom to make a very attractive card.

The impression of looking through the trellis arch gives this picture an added dimension.

Covering this dark red card with a piece of pink bobble net turns a very plain card into a stunning creation. Red eyelets have been inserted at the right-hand corners and a piece of pale pink ribbon tied through the upper eyelet. This offsets the darkness of the card and creates an elegant look.

A strip of yellow card mounted on to a dark green card and adorned with two beautiful butterflies gives this card a springtime effect. Add a dab of glitter to the butterfly wings for that little bit of extra glamour.

Mat mounting blue on a silver-speckled cream card gives added depth to the image. Coiled wire is used to hold the tags which are trimmed with little pink flowers. You could always place your greeting on to the tag, as it will make the card that little bit different.

...ming Beautiful

...en identical prints a lot of detail and depth can be accomplished with this picture. When completed you will see the depth between the flowers looking through to the branch.

When cutting out multiple flowers store each flower separately in envelopes so that no pieces are lost. This also keeps all the parts of each flower in one place for convenience when you are making them up.

The shaping of the flowers is particularly important as nature provides them with lots of curves, so try to reproduce that natural look. I hope you enjoy creating this stunner!

You will need

- Seven Cherry Blossom large prints
- Craft knife
- Cutting mat
- Silicone sealant
- Shaping tools
- Eraser
- Foam pad
- Cocktail sticks
- Tweezers
- Fine tweezers
- Card frame and masking tape
- Envelopes

Note

You would not normally cut a hole in the base print, but in this case it will be covered by the next stage and saves using a whole print for a single leaf.

1. Take the first print and cut the leaf out on the middle left, then put the print safely to one side. This will be your base print.

2. Take the second print and cut out the background areas in between the leaves and flowers.

3. Now cut away the background around the leaves and flowers.

4. Take the third print and cut out the upper left flower (when looking from the top). Put it safely to one side.

Tip

When assembling the picture, place the base print on to a piece of thick cardboard. This provides a rigid base to work on. You can discard the cardboard once the picture is completed.

5. Still using the third print, cut out the flower on the middle right (again when looking from the top) and put it safely to one side.

6. Cut out the two flowers at the bottom as one shape – do not cut the two apart where they overlap. Put it to one side.

7. Cut away the background and dark green areas within the remaining group of flowers and buds at the top of the third print.

8. Cut out the entire group of flowers and buds as one shape.

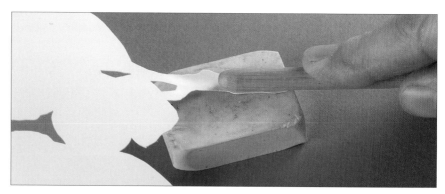

9. Take the piece from the second print and gently turn the leaves with the barrel of the shaping tool so they curl backwards.

10. Place the branch of the piece on to an eraser and run the barrel gently up and down it to give the branch a rounded shape as shown.

11. Place the silicone sealant in the centre of the large areas of the piece as shown.

Tip

Make sure that you keep the lid of the silicone sealant on when it is not in use.

12. Carefully pick up the piece with tweezers and place it on top of the base print.

13. Make any necessary adjustments to the positioning with a cocktail stick, then leave the silicone to dry thoroughly.

14. Take the leaf from the base print and shape it on the foam pad.

15. Apply some silicone to the back of the leaf.

16. Place the leaf at an angle, making sure that the part overcut with the petals lies flush with the layer below.

17. Gently shape the top left flower using the barrel of the shaping tool, as before.

18. Apply silicone sealant to the flower and place it on the picture. Use a cocktail stick to make any small adjustments that are necessary.

19. Shape the middle right flower, then apply silicone and place it on the picture.

20. Repeat the process of shaping, applying silicone sealant and placing to add the pair of flowers at the bottom of the picture.

Cherry Blossoms 1 by Reina

21. Shape, apply silicone to and place the remaining group of flowers and buds at the top. This completes the basic picture.

22. Take the remaining prints and carefully cut out all of the pieces marked below in orange, then all the pieces marked in green, then all the pieces marked in purple, then all the pieces marked in red, and finally all of the pieces marked in blue. Put each group of pieces carefully in a separate envelope.

Fourth print

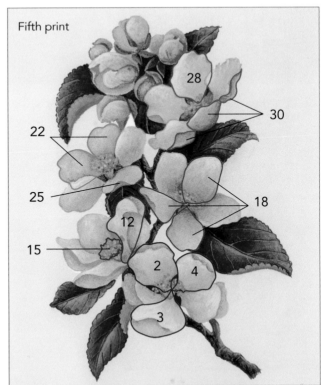

Fifth print

Sixth print

Seventh print

23. Starting with the piece marked 1 from the fourth print, begin to assemble the flower at the bottom. Shape the petals from the fifth print (marked 2, 3 and 4), apply silicone and place them as shown.

24. Shape the larger petal from the sixth print (marked 5), apply silicone and place the end of the petal flush with the centre of the flower, tucking it below the petal marked 4.

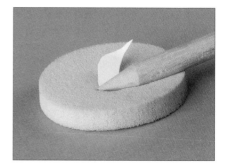

25. Shape the small petal edge from the sixth print (marked 6) by rolling the pointed end of the shaping tool over the petal. Use the foam pad to support the piece while it is being shaped.

26. Smear a little silicone on each end and a small dab in the centre of the petal edge, then use the tweezers to place it. Turn the flower to make it easier to place the piece, if necessary.

27. Take the petal edges from the seventh print (all marked 7) and shape them by holding them with the tweezers and gently easing the ends back with your fingers.

28. Smear silicone to the ends and a dab in the centre of each petal edge and place them one by one on the flower.

29. Shape the stamen from the seventh print (8) with the rounded end of the shaping tool. Use the eraser to support the piece while you shape it.

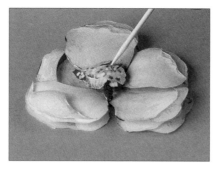

30. Apply a dab of silicone and place the stamen in the centre of the flower as shown.

31. Complete the flower by shaping the top of the stamen (piece 9 from the sixth print), then applying silicone and placing it on top of piece 8.

32. Assemble the flower on the lower left, using pieces 10–15. Shape the petals, petal edges and stamens as for the first flower.

33. Assemble the flower on the middle right, using pieces 16–20. Again, shape the pieces in the same way as the other flowers.

34. Shape, apply silicone to and place pieces 21–26 to assemble the flower on the top left.

35. Assemble the final flower using pieces 27–32, shaping, applying silicone to and placing the pieces as for the others.

36. Cut out a complete bud from any of the prints and shape it in the same way as a face (see page 16 for the technique) to give the bud a nice round effect.

37. Using another print, cut out the petals from the same bud, and shape them in the same way. Smear a little silicone on to the back of the petal and place to complete the bud.

38. Make up the other buds in the same way. Some of the larger buds may require three pieces.

39. Cut out the twig and the curled up edges of the leaves. Shape the twig by running the barrel of the shaping tool gently up it to give it a slight curve.

40. Apply silicone to the back of the leaf edges and three smallest buds and use tweezers to place them on the picture.

41. Apply silicone and place the remaining buds.

42. Apply silicone to the back of the twig and smear a little on the very bottom. Place the twig, making sure that the end lies flush with the layer below. Working from the top down, apply silicone to the flowers and place them one by one.

43. Allow the piece to dry thoroughly and use masking tape at the back to secure it to the card frame.

Opposite:
This spray of blossom looks as though it has just been freshly picked from the tree! Surrounded in a dark green and cream mount, this makes a wonderful picture.

Leisa

Hibiscus Blooms

The bluish mauve of the hibiscus flowers entwined with dainty pinks, all encompassed within a green mount creates this pleasing picture. The leaf at the bottom is gently falling over the mount, leading the eye to the main flower, which is the focal point and raised higher than the rest.

Abundance of Flowers

An array of mauves and whites, this picture is complemented by the cream and dusty lilac mounts. The flowers are mounted at different heights and angles to give this picture a natural look.

A Rainbow of Colours

This stunning picture shows how the cutting of fine delicate stems together with the gentle curves of the petals enhances the three-dimensional effect. The blue flower is lifted and tilted to give the picture depth and the colour of the mounts complements the green foliage.

Rob. Pohl
F

Scrambled Eggs

Identify the parts of the picture that you would like to emphasise and make a note of them before you start cutting. By paying attention to the small details, you can turn an average picture into something special.

When making a picture involving people or objects standing on a floor, the floor should be angled upwards or the people or objects angled down to the floor to avoid an odd 'levitating' appearance.

1. Set aside print one as the base print, then cut out the whole chef from print two and set him aside safely.

2. Cut out the hat, right forearm, left shoulder, tunic and floor from print three as shown above. Put the pieces safely to one side.

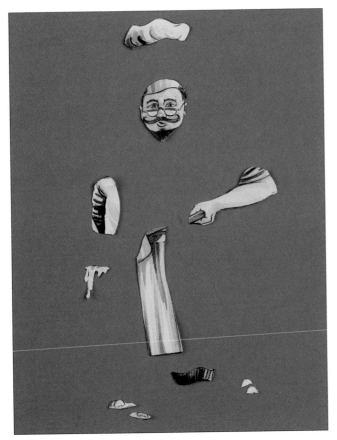

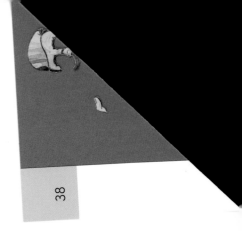

3. Carefully cut out the top of the hat, the chef's face, his left forearm and elbow, his right shoulder, the front of his apron, the trouser cuff and the eggs spilling from his pan from print four; then cut out the two egg shells on the right, and the two broken eggs on the left.

4. Take print five and cut out the chef's spectacles, neckerchief, spoon and handle; then cut out the rolled-up sleeve on his left arm, his trouser leg, both egg shells on the left and finally, the pair of broken eggs on the right. Cut this last piece out as one item.

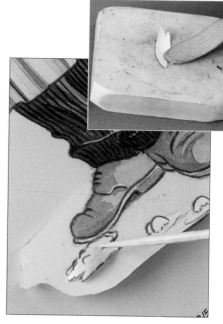

5. Take print six and cut out the chef's thumb, the neckerchief, his forehead, nose and moustache (cutting into the hat-rim), the front of the pan, the spilled eggs on the floor and the turnup of his trouser cuff.

6. Take the floor piece from print three, apply silicone to the back and place it on the base print. Angle the piece so that the back of the floor is flush with the base print.

7. Gently curve the spilled eggs from print six with the spoon-shaped end of the shaping tool as shown in the inset. Then smear a little silicone on to the back of the eggs and place on to the floor.

8. Place silicone on to the chef on the base print as shown.

9. Take the whole chef (from print two) and smear a little silicone over his feet before placing him on to the base print. Make sure that the soles of his feet are flush with the floor.

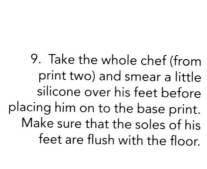

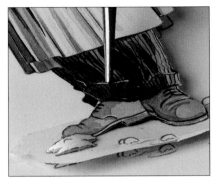

10. Place the turnup on the chef's right leg, making sure the bottom is flat against his ankle.

11. Shape the chef's right shoulder from print four with the barrel of the shaping tool, apply silicone and place it, making sure that it lies flush with his chest on the right-hand side as shown.

12. Shape the edges of the chef's left trouser leg with the barrel of the shaping tool, apply silicone and place it.

13. Put a slight curve on the tunic from print three, then put a small piece of silicone at the top and two larger pieces at the bottom before placing it.

14. Smear some silicone at the top of the apron (print four) and add two dabs of silicone at the bottom before placing it. This piece breaks up the flatness of the apron.

15. Use the barrel of the shaping tool to shape the chef's right forearm (from print three), then apply silicone to his elbow and hand and place, making sure that his elbow is flush with his upper arm.

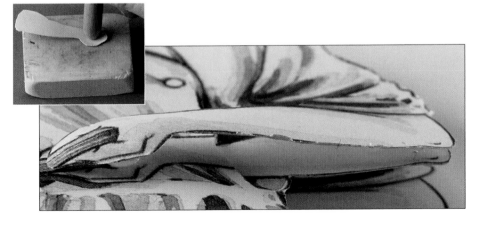

16. Shape the chef's lower left arm with the barrel of the shaping tool, then use the round end of the shaping tool to add a curve to his hand (inset). Add silicone and place. The sleeve and the panhandle should be flush with the surface, forming an arch as shown.

17. Shape the upper part of his left sleeve (from print three) using the barrel of the shaping tool, apply silicone and place.

18. Smear a little silicone on to the pan handle (print five) and a dab in the middle of the pan. Stick the handle down first, then place the pan.

19. Hold the top of the pan with the tweezers and use your fingers to give it a slight curve. Smear silicone down both sides and place it.

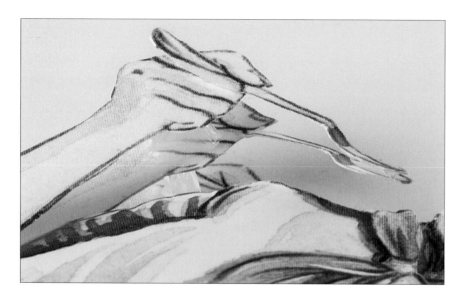

Tip

You can use a cocktail stick to adjust pieces after they have been placed. This makes getting the piece 'just right' much easier.

20. Use angled tweezers to hold the spoon while you smear silicone on to the centre of his right forearm and the bowl of the spoon. Place a dab of silicone on the back of his hand and place the piece with the elbow and bowl of the spoon flush with the piece below.

21. Use long tweezers to hold the neckerchief (from print six) while you smear silicone on the knot and at the two top corners, then place it.

22. Shape the chef's face (from print four), apply silicone and place it.

23. Smear a thin layer of silicone over the eggs spilling from the pan (print four) and place.

24. Hold the chef's left sleeve cuff with your tweezers and gently shape it with your fingers, then apply silicone in the centre of the piece and smearing a little on each end. Place the piece.

25. Shape the chef's forehead and hat-rim piece as you would a face, then smear silicone to the hat-rim and place, making sure that the hat-rim is flush with the layer below and the nose is a little raised.

26. Use the barrel of the shaping tool to add a slight curve to the hat (from print three). Smear silicone on to the bottom and a small dab at the top, then place the piece bottom first as shown.

27. Hold the spectacles from print five with the angled tweezers, smear silicone on the back of each of the lenses, then place them on the chef's nose.

28. Shape the top of the hat with the barrel of the shaping tool, then smear silicone on the top edge and place it.

Tip

If a piece will not come off the tweezers, use a cocktail stick to coax it off.

29. Add a smear of silicone to the neckerchief from print five and place.

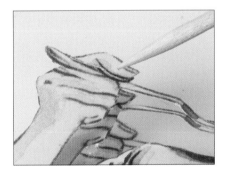

30. Smear silicone on the back of the thumb (from print six) and place.

31. Pick up the turnup of the chef's left trouser leg (from print six) with the tweezers and gently shape it with your fingers. Smear a little silicone on to both ends of the turnup and place it.

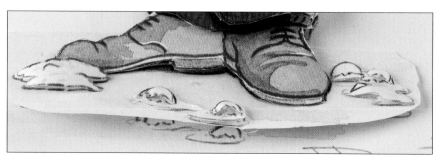

32. Use the pointed end of the shaping tool to make the eggs and eggshells slightly rounded.

33. Smear a little silicone on the back of each of the broken eggs and eggshells, and place to complete the picture.

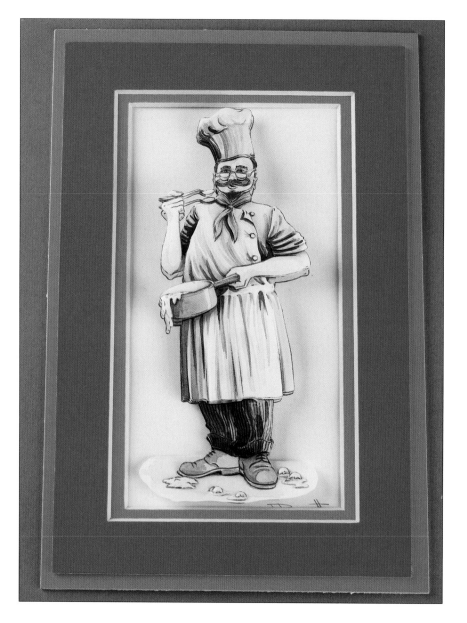

34. Place the frame carefully over the completed picture to finish.

Opposite:

Set in a double mount, the eye is directed to the saucepan and down to the eggs on the floor by the chef's feet. He looks as though he is just about to walk through the doorway with that messy pan of eggs!

I Hereby Sentence You To...

The learned judge, resplendent in his judicial robes, is just about to pass sentence, having referred to all his law books which are set outside the mount. The shield and motto have been cut out to give this part of the picture extra interest. Note how the colour of the mount sets off the picture.

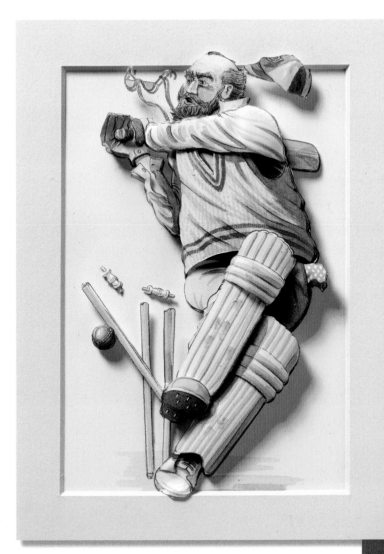

Howzat!

This cricketer is about to swing the bat and hit the ball, but far too late. Instead of raising the floor, his foot is resting on the edge of the cream mount and his head is slightly above the mount. These details help to create the effect that he is moving forward to hit the ball.

Fore by Fore

You can tell by the lumps of grass that are flying that our golfer has had many failed attempts to hit the golf ball. No need to lift the floor on this picture as the golfer is leaning forward and his feet rest naturally on the floor. Framed within a dark green mount he looks at home on the golf course. Now – if only he could hit that ball!

Sweet Dreams

Using rubber stamps is a very creative way to make three-dimensional cards and it is especially satisfying if you enjoy colouring or painting. They have the advantage that you can colour as many images as you need. The same stamp can be used to make a variety of cards by changing the colours and backgrounds.

Colour in one image first; if you do not like it, stamp another one and try again until you find the colours you like. Keep the colouring simple and you will be surprised at how well the picture turns out.

You will need

- Two sheets of A4 white card
- Solvent ink pad and Fairy stamp
- Stamping mat
- Double-ended felt tip pens: light pink, dark pink, red, light green, dark green, yellow, light brown
- Paintbrush and sheet of acetate
- Glaze and brush cleaner
- Craft knife and cutting mat
- Glitter and glitter tray
- Scissors
- Shaping tools, eraser and foam pad
- Card blank 20 x 20cm (8 x 8in)
- Edging strip
- Tweezers
- Silicone sealant
- Foam squares

1. Ink the fairy stamp by pressing it firmly down on the ink pad, then press it firmly down on to paper five times to make five identical images.

2. Take the sheet of acetate and use the dark pink felt tip pen to draw a small square on it. The ink will remain wet on the acetate, so you can use it as a palette.

3. Pick up the ink with a paintbrush and paint the fairy's dress on the first image. Add extra ink on the folds and shadows of the dress by painting on a second layer of ink.

Tip

I use watercolour pens as I find them easy to apply, but you could just as easily use paints or pencils.

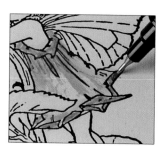

4. Use the fine tip of the pen to darken the trims and hem of the dress. You do not need to be particularly accurate with your colouring because the pieces will be cut out.

5. Draw a square on the acetate with the yellow felt tip pen, and then use a paintbrush to paint the ink over the whole picture apart from the fairy.

6. Use the thick end of the light pink pen to colour in the fairy's arm, legs and face, then vary the colour on the roses with the light pink pen.

7. Use the red pen with the acetate palette and the brush to paint the lower left rose and the rosebud on the bottom right.

8. Use the thicker end of the red pen to add strength to the colour of the rose at the base.

9. Mix the light and dark green inks on the acetate, and use the mix to paint all of the leaves on the plant.

10. Use the yellow pen to strengthen the base of the fairy's wings, and use the light brown pen to paint her hair.

11. Finish the first picture by colouring the stem of the rose with the light brown pen.

12. Colour the other pictures in the same way. Do not worry too much about making them all identical – this is part of the charm of the piece.

13. Use scissors to cut a square around each of the pictures and put them to one side. Take the first picture and use the craft knife to remove the blank background, starting from the middle as shown.

14. Continue to cut away the background from the first piece until it is all gone, then repeat the process for the second picture.

15. Place dabs of silicone on to the back of the first piece and position it approximately 5mm (¼in) on top of the second to make the first layer of the picture.

16. Cut the following pieces from the third picture: the fairy's body; the edges of the top rose and the leaves below it; the red rosebud and the leaf near it; the top of the rose at the bottom. Put each piece safely to one side.

17. Cut the following pieces from the fourth picture: centre from the top rose and the large petal from the same rose; the hem and sleeve frill of the dress, the stem and calyx of the red rose; the centre of the rose at the bottom; the leaf that lies across the fairy's dress; the calyx of the rose bud; the leaves near the rosebud. Put each piece safely to one side.

18. Cut the following pieces from the fifth picture: the fairy's wing (cut into the shoulder and dress as shown); the fairy's face; her back leg (cutting through the front foot); the front petal from the rose at the bottom; the front petal of the red rose; the front petal and the curled edge of the top rose; the stem of the rose, overcutting where necessary to keep it as one long piece.

19. Use the barrel of the shaping tool to give the fairy's leg (from the fifth picture) a slight curve, then add silicone sealant to the back and place it.

20. Apply silicone directly on to the first layer of the picture at the side of the top leaf, the middle leaf that overlaps the fairy, and the bottom-most leaf, then place the stem (see inset).

21. Gently round the tips of the wing (from the fifth picture) with the barrel of shaping tool, apply silicone to the back and place.

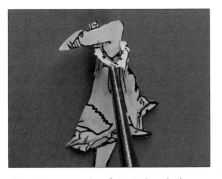

22. Prepare the fairy's body by smearing silicone on to the dress frill and placing it; then smear silicone on to the sleeve frill and place it by tucking it under the fairy's arm. Put the body to one side to dry.

23. Shape, apply silicone to and place all of the individual leaves (from the third and fourth pictures), except for the central leaf that overlaps the fairy's dress.

24. Apply silicone to and place the red rose, the rosebud and the rose at the bottom (all from the third picture).

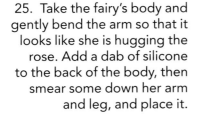

25. Take the fairy's body and gently bend the arm so that it looks like she is hugging the rose. Add a dab of silicone to the back of the body, then smear some down her arm and leg, and place it.

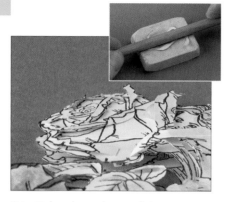

26. Take the edges of the top rose (from the third picture), and shape them with the barrel of the shaping tool (as shown in the inset). Be very gentle as they are fragile. Smear silicone on the largest areas on the back, and place the edges.

27. Add a small dab of silicone to the back of the leaf that overlaps the fairy's dress and put it carefully in place.

28. Put a dab of silicone on to the back of the top rose's large petal (from the fourth picture) and place it; then overlay the front petal of the top rose (from the fifth picture).

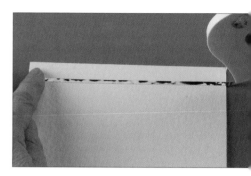

29. Shape the face, add silicone and place; then shape and place the centre of the top rose (fourth picture) before doing the same with the edges of the top rose (from the third picture).

30. Shape and place the calyx of the red rose, then shape and place the centre of the bottom rose (both of these pieces are from the fourth picture) and then the front petal from the rose at the bottom (fifth picture).

31. Take the card blank and run the edging strip in a straight line across the card, about 2½cm (1in) from the edge.

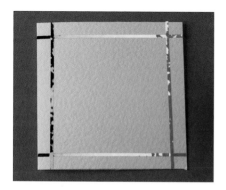

32. Repeat this on the other three sides.

33. Use a brush to paint glaze on to the fairy's wings and various parts of the leaves and flowers. While the glaze is wet, put the finished picture into the glitter tray, sprinkle glitter over the picture and leave to dry.

34. Apply sticky foam pads to the back of the fairy and then remove the backing with the blade of the craft knife.

35. Place the finished picture in the centre of the card.

This rose fairy is dreamily caressing the delicate rose. A metallic silver edging strip accentuates the light tone of the cream embossed card.

Is it Raining?

This nasturtium fairy is sitting outside the window wondering if his umbrella will keep him dry. This is a cream embossed card with a round aperture. A circle of terracotta card with acetate film inside it creates the impression of a window. Strips of terracotta card were run down the left and bottom edges and the card is finished with a pale green insert.

Sweet Lilac

This lilac fairy is mounted on a ring of purple card, trimmed with frayed purple stranded silk, surrounded by a piece of white vellum with purple dots. This was then mounted on to a purple card blank.

Hide and Seek

The iris fairy is hiding among the flowers away from the dragonflies. The picture is set against a deep green backing card, then mounted on to a delicate flower-patterned parchment paper. This is then secured on to a plain white card, which makes a striking combination. The dragonflies are made from outline stickers.

Hello Mr Bee

The clover fairy is busy helping the bee to collect the pollen. This is a very simple picture that has been stamped, coloured and then cut into an irregular shape. The edges have then been coloured and smudged before the picture was mounted on to a maroon velvet card blank. The contrast between the white and the maroon is very eye-catching. Glitter was sprinkled into the glaze on the fairy's wings while it was still wet to achieve the glittery effect.

ver Alert

g three-dimensional pictures of animals it is very important that no gaps are visible where limbs join the body. I picked this print as I can clearly illustrate the advantage of using a repositionable low-tack tape to keep the limbs close to the body to ensure a lifelike finish.

This picture also shows the necessity of furring the animal to give a realistic look, so make sure that your blade is sharp before starting. There are very few pieces to cut out from the prints – the skill to obtaining a truly lifelike picture is in the assembly.

1. Set one print aside as the base print, then cut the background away from print two as shown.

2. Cut out the whole leopard from print three, cutting up into the base of the tail to the top of the leopard's rump. Cut out the knothole of the tree.

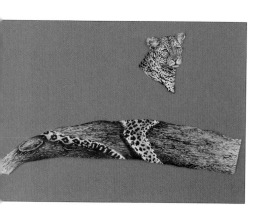

3. Take print four, and cut out the leopard's head and neck as one piece, then cut out the main trunk of the tree, overcutting the leopard's leg and tail as shown.

4. Cut out the leopard's head, the front leg and the rear leg from print five.

5. Cut the 'face' of the leopard from print six, feathering the whiskers. Then cut out the branches on the left, overcutting the leopard's tail where necessary. Finally, cut out the front piece of bark, overcutting the leopard's leg and tail, as shown.

6. Take the leopard from print three, and cut out the eyes as one piece.

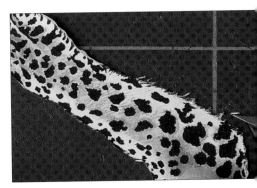

7. Fur the belly where the leopard's foreleg meets the body.

8. Take the leopard's head from print five and fur the inside of the left ear.

9. Fur the bottom of the leg from print five.

10. Take the leopard's face from print six and fur the inside of the right ear.

11. Use the pointed end of the shaping tool to shape the eyes (from step 6).

12. Place the eyes on a piece of low-tack tape to hold them in place, then use a cocktail stick to apply a spot of glaze to each eye. Set the piece aside to dry.

13. Take the piece from print two, apply silicone to the back of the leopard and the main trunk and then place the piece. Note that you should not apply silicone to the smaller branches.

14. Turn the picture upside-down and smear silicone under the tips of the branches, then press them down gently until they stick flush with the background.

15. Shape the left-hand branch from print six with the barrel of the shaping tool.

16. Smear silicone down the biggest parts of the branch, then place it, making sure the base of the piece is flush with the main trunk.

17. Use a little low-tack tape along the join at the trunk to hold the branch in place while the silicone dries.

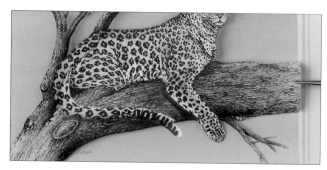

18. Remove the tape after five minutes, then give the main trunk from print four a slight curve with your fingers, apply silicone and place it.

19. Apply dabs of silicone to the trunk on the main picture.

20. Give the large piece of bark from print six a slight curve with your fingers and smear silicone on to the ends.

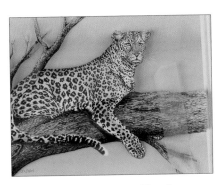

21. Place the piece of bark and use a piece of low-tack tape to hold it in place until the silicone dries.

22. Take the knothole from print three, smear silicone on to the back and place it.

23. Apply silicone to the body, mouth and foreleg of the leopard on the main picture.

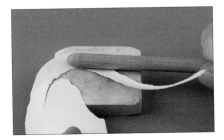

24. Take the leopard from print three and run the barrel of the shaping tool up the leopard's tail to give it a slight curve.

25. Place the leopard.

26. Shape and apply silicone to the front leg from print five. Place it, and then use tape to hold the top of the leg flush with the body.

27. While the foreleg is drying, shape the rear leg from print five as you would a face, apply silicone and place it. You may need to lift the tail a little to get it in place.

28. Apply a tiny dab of silicone under the tail to secure and support it, then use a little low-tack tape to hold it while the silicone dries.

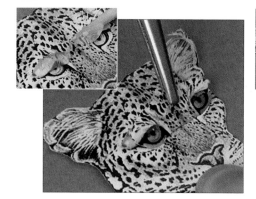

29. Take the face from print five, shape the cheeks as you would a face, then add a dab of silicone just above the eyes (inset). Place the glazed eyes from step 12, tilting them to ensure that they are flush with the face at the bottom.

30. Shape the 'face' from print six by folding the nose gently around your tweezers (inset), then apply silicone and place it on top of the head. This completes the face, so set it to one side to dry.

31. Remove all of the tape from the main picture, and shape the head and neck from print four. Apply silicone to the piece, smearing it along the top of the neck and where it joins the body, and apply. Use low-tack tape to secure it while the silicone dries.

32. Apply silicone to the back of the completed face and place it. This completes the picture.

33. Allow to dry and remove the low-tack tape to finish. Place the card frame around the picture and secure with masking tape on the back.

The leopard, always watchful, is sitting alert on the branch of a tree with his hindlegs curled up beneath him. His tail is gently shaped and trailing along the treetrunk. The branch directly above the leopard has been offset to give the background slightly more detail. Notice how the decoupage brings out the subtle folds in the leopard's neck. The whole picture has been framed within a double mount of cream and green to complement the colours of the animal itself.

Resting

This cheetah was made using the same techniques as for the leopard.
Again, it was framed in a double mount on cream and green.

King of Beasts

The lion is renowned for his magnificent mane and to create that beautiful mass of hair requires patience, a great deal of time and at least two craft knife blades. He has a beautiful face and really does look like the king of beasts.

Lazing in the Sun

This tiger is happily reclining on the grass by a tree. To make him look as though he is resting in the grass it is necessary to glue and tape the bottom of his body down flat to the ground and tilt the top of his body slightly forwards away from the tree.

Masque

Outline stickers can make distinctive three-dimensional cards. They require very little (if any) shaping, so they make quick, easy cards. Colouring in is optional – sometimes it is better to leave the pieces plain. Another option is to put the stickers on to coloured rather than plain card.

This mask outline sticker creates a very striking card. I have emphasised the facial qualities by minimising the colouring.

You will need

- Four mask outline sticker sheets
- White card
- Double-ended felt tip pens: light orange, dark orange and yellow
- Craft knife and cutting mat
- Card blank
- Velvet paper 10.5 x 10.5cm (4 x 4in)
- Velvet paper 13.5 x 13.5cm (5¼ x 5¼in)
- Fancy-edged gold card 12 x 12cm (4¾ x 4¾in)
- Glue dots
- Tweezers
- Silicone sealant

1. Carefully peel off the mask sticker from the backing, and lay it face down on the table, so the sticky side is facing you.

2. Peel off three more and lay them face down side-by-side.

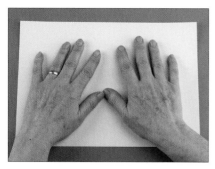

3. Take an A4 sheet of white card and carefully place it over all four stickers. Press down gently to secure the stickers.

4. Turn the card over and make sure that all the masks are stuck firmly on to the card.

5. Use the thick end of the light orange pen to colour in the parts of the mask shown above.

6. Use the thick end of the dark orange pen to colour in the flower petals on the mask.

7. Colour the centres of the flowers and the middle of the head band with the thick end of the yellow pen.

8. Colour the other faces in the same way.

9. Cut the card into sections, with a mask on each.

10. Cut carefully around one of the masks, removing the excess card.

11. Cut out the inner pieces of background card, cutting around the spirals carefully until you are left with the mask shown.

12. Take the second mask and cut away the curl on the right-hand side as shown.

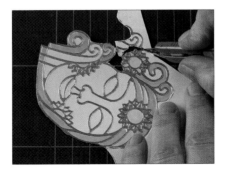

13. Continue cutting around the second mask, cutting away the small curl below the flower on the left-hand side.

14. Cut the rest of the background away, then carefully cut away the small areas of background that are enclosed by the spirals.

15. Take the third mask and cut out the areas of the face shown above. Be careful to cut right up to, but not through, the outline sticker itself.

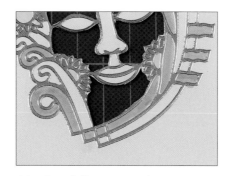

16. Carefully cut out the area below the chin, cutting through the outline sticker where necessary.

17. Cut away the background and everything around the face except for the white spiral and the small flower on the left.

18. Cut the flower from the forehead of the final mask and set it aside.

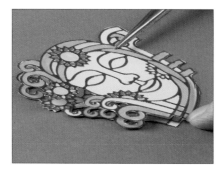

19. Apply silicone to the back of the second mask and place it on top of the first.

20. Apply silicone to the back of the third mask and place it on top of the second.

21. Apply silicone to the back of the flower from the final mask and place it on the forehead. This completes the picture.

22. Take the larger piece of velvet paper and lay it face-down on the table.

23. Run a line of glue dots down the edges of the velvet paper.

24. Press the velvet paper on to the card blank.

25. Apply glue dots to the edges of the fancy-edged gold card and place it in the centre of the velvet paper.

26. Apply glue dots to the edges of the back of the smaller piece of velvet paper and place it in the centre of the fancy-edged gold card.

27. Take one of the discarded sticker backs and remove the small mask from below the big mask, leaving the small dots behind. Pick up one of these small dots on the end of your craft knife.

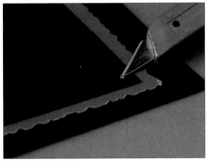

28. Place the dot on the corner of the smaller piece of velvet paper.

29. Repeat this until there is a small dot in each of the corners of the velvet paper.

30. Apply silicone to the back of the mask picture and place it on the card.

The dark blue velvet set against the gold enhances the beauty of this sticker. Leaving the face white adds depth to the piece. The colouring on the rest of the outline stickers shows the impact that can be made through the use of even a small amount of colour.

Happy Days

This solid black vintage car is given a three-dimensional effect by using three identical outline stickers. It is enhanced by edging a piece of gold card with gold and silver ribbon which is then mounted on to a cream embossed card blank. This was decorated with balloon stickers (held in place with double-sided foam squares) and the car sticker was placed in the centre. This would make an ideal card for a wedding or anniversary.

Tulips and Butterflies

This picture was made with four identical outline stickers on white card. The gold pieces on the tulips and leaves were added after the glue was dry and were made from the scraps that are left behind when the sticker is peeled from the sheet. Placed on to a plain gold card with double-sided tape and decorated with butterfly outline stickers, this makes a simple and effective card.

Delicate Daisies

Four outline stickers were used on this card. Small pieces of parchment paper are placed behind the stickers – orange for the flowers and pale green for the leaves. The card was made by cutting out two squares of orange card with craft scissors to give a fancy edge, then placing them at an angle on to a cream linen-effect card. The round pieces of outline sticker left behind from the centre of the flowers were then placed on each corner of the orange squares and dark orange ribbon was run down each side.

Springtime

This card was made from four identical outline stickers placed on to a white backing card. The white background was cut away from one of the pictures and the remaining three used to create the three-dimensional image. This was then mounted on to a gold card trimmed with white and gold braid.

You're Late!

This street scene is reminiscent of days gone by, with muted colours and lines of washing strung between windows.

Cutting out the window panes gives depth to the buildings. This effect is enhanced by the shadows cast by the walls in the finished piece.

This type of picture is probably the hardest to create three-dimensionally as the buildings must be positioned exactly for the required effect, but following the steps carefully will produce a wonderful three-dimensional picture.

You will need

- Six Visiting Grandma prints
- Craft knife, scissors and cutting mat
- Shaping tools, eraser and foam pad
- Low-tack tape
- Ruler
- Tweezers
- Silicone sealant
- Foam squares
- Card frame
- Clear waterbased adhesive
- Thick cardboard
- Scrap paper 20 x 10cm (8 x 4in)

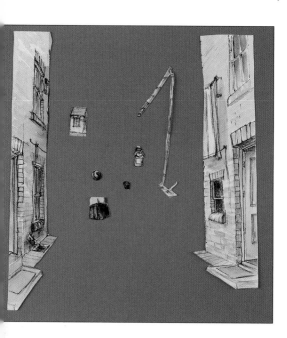

1. Take six identical prints, set one aside as the base print, then cut these main parts from print two: left side wall, including doorstep and paving stones; right side wall, including doorstep and paving stones; and then cut out these extras – mother's skirt, mother's hat, grandma, child's hat, the back drain and pipes and the top floor of the back building.

2. From print three, cut out the single main part on this print – the top washing line including the washing. Cut out the extras, starting from the left: left doorstep, door top, window sill, drain, top window sill and the roofs of two central buildings. From the middle: the roof of the top back building. From the right-hand side: downpipe, bottom back window, top window ledge, bottom window, front bottom window ledge, top of the bottom window, top window ledge, right doorstep, door and door top.

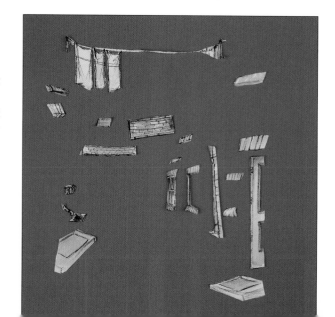

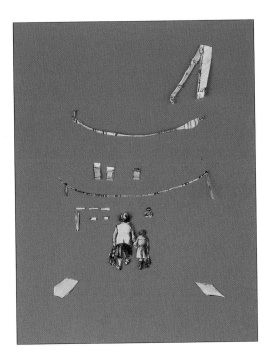

3. From print four, cut out these main parts: middle washing line, bottom washing line, and the mother and child as one piece. Cut out the following extras: left door, left door top; middle door top, middle door central plank; right door top, right door central plank; top of the gutter and downpipe, grandma's head and arms, background chimney stacks, left-hand main door mat and the right-hand main door mat.

4. Cut away the distant buildings, sky and washing lines from print five, then cut the three pieces of washing out of the discarded piece.

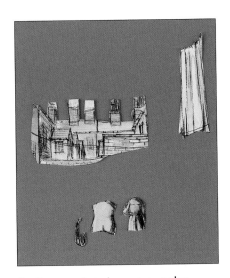

5. From print six, cut out the distant buildings, overcutting the nearer rooftops where necessary; then cut out the washing on the right, then mother's jacket, mother's bag and the child's coat.

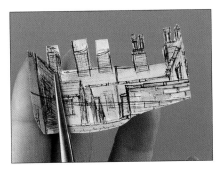

6. Pick up the distant buildings from print six with your tweezers on the corner, and fold the shaded area towards you.

7. Apply silicone to the back of the piece and place it on to the base print. Put a piece of thick cardboard behind the base print to support it and hold it up to ensure the lines are aligned correctly. Adjust with a cocktail stick if necessary.

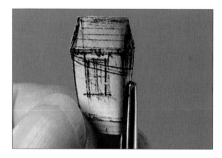

8. Take the top floor of the back building from print two, and fold the part in shadow away from you with the tweezers.

9. Apply silicone to the centre of this piece and place into position.

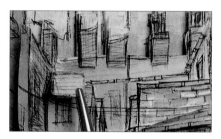

10. Apply silicone to the three chimney stacks (from print four) and position them. Apply silicone to the roof of the top floor at the back of the building cut from print three and position.

11. Take the main piece from print five and cut out the panes of glass from the window on the left of the large piece of washing.

12. Repeat this on the other windows; then cut out the shadowed parts behind the doors as shown.

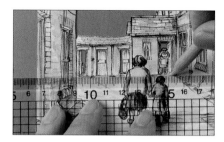

13. Use a ruler and the pointed end of the shaping tool to score a line from the left-most edge of the picture along the bottom of the building to the corner of the street below grandma.

14. Score a similar line from this corner to the edge of the front wall, following the line above the drain to the right front wall.

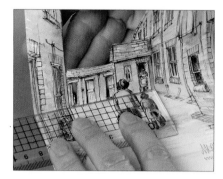

15. Using the ruler to help, fold the piece forward along the scorelines, being careful not to crease the piece beyond the corner where the scorelines meet or beyond the drainpipe by the right front wall.

16. Apply silicone to the base print as shown and leave it to cure for three minutes. Do not apply any silicone on the bottom half of the picture. While it is drying, fold the scrap paper in half. Place it at the bottom of the base print, with the fold level with the foreground doorstep. Secure it with low-tack tape.

17. Now place the piece from print five, allowing the scrap card to support the street at an angle. Allow the picture to dry thoroughly.

18. Starting with the building to the left of grandma's house, take the door lintels, open door and the two central planks of the other doors (all from print four). Smear a little silicone to the back of each piece and place in turn. Once these are placed, apply the roof of the building from print three, making sure the top of the roof is flush with the background.

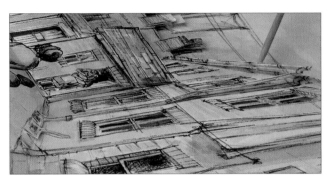

19. Take the roof of grandma's house (from print three), apply silicone to the middle of the piece and place it so that the top is flush with the background. Apply silicone and place grandma (from print two), then run the barrel of the shaping tool up grandma's head and arms (from print four) to give the piece a slight curve, smear some silicone on the back and place it.

20. From print two, take the back guttering/drainpipe/drain piece and apply silicone to the guttering. Apply a little of the waterbased glue on the drain and place. This ensures that the drain is flat on the background while the guttering and drainpipe remain raised. Place this piece very carefully as the glue dries almost instantaneously.

21. Apply silicone to the window sills and the surround of the front lower windows (print three) and place. Take the bottom half of the front drainpipe (print three), and attach with waterbased glue at the bottom and silicone at the top.

22. Shape the guttering (from print four) with the barrel of the shaping tool, apply silicone and place it.

23. Take the wall pieces from print two and cut out the upper window panes from the left wall and all of the window panes on the right wall, then cut out the top and bottom parts of the open doorway on the right.

24. Use the pointed end of the shaping tool and the ruler to score along both of these pieces where the doorsteps meet the walls; then fold the pavements forwards as shown.

25. Apply silicone to the back of the walls, and waterbased glue to the pavements, then place.

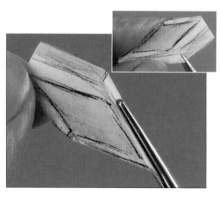

26. Take the right-hand doorstep from print three and cut to the edge of the step as shown in the inset, then use the tweezers to fold the edges down to form a box shape.

27. Apply silicone and place the doorstep.

28. From print three, take both window sills on the right-hand side, the window lintel, the door lintel and the front of the door. Apply silicone and place each piece in turn.

29. From print three, take the window sills for both windows on the left-hand wall and the door lintel. Apply silicone and place each in turn. Shape the doorstep as for the right-hand wall then place the doorstep. Finally, use silicone and waterbased glue to attach the drain/overflow pipe.

30. From print three, take the washing line and washing. Apply waterbased glue to the back of the left end, then add silicone to the back of the right end and under each piece of washing and place. Take the middle and bottom washing line from print four, smear silicone on all four ends and place.

31. Take the three pieces of washing from print five and give them a slight curve with the barrel of the shaping tool. Apply silicone to the backs and place carefully, making sure that the tops of the washing are flush with the washing line itself.

32. Take the doormats from print four, smear silicone on the backs and place on the doorsteps. Next shape the mother and child piece by running the barrel of the shaping tool up each character vertically to give them a slight curve. Apply silicone to their backs and waterbased glue to their feet and place them.

33. Cut out the centre of the child's coat from print six.

34. Shape mother's skirt from print two, apply silicone and place so that the top is flush with the bottom of the jacket.

35. Shape her hat with the point of the shaping tool, then apply silicone to it and her handbag (both from print two) and place. Add a slight curve to mother's jacket (print six), add silicone and place.

36. Give both parts of the child's coat a slight curve, then apply silicone and place. Shape the child's head from print two in the same way as mother's hat, then apply silicone and place it.

37. Remove the thin piece of card supporting the street, then apply silicone near the fold and support it until the silicone dries. This completes the picture.

Tip
The placing of card underneath the road is very important as this allows movement so that the buildings and people can be correctly aligned.

38. Secure the card frame around the picture with masking tape to finish.

Opposite:
There is a lot of detail in this finished picture which captures the period perfectly: narrow streets and a time when you lived near enough to walk to grandma's. The mounts of marbled grey and light grey further enhance the picture.

VISITING GRANDMA'S

Piano Practice

'I may be reading the paper, but I am listening!' This picture is reminiscent of the days when a piano was the main source of entertainment and children were encouraged to play. The right side wall has been tilted forward and the floor raised to give perspective to the room. This allows the piano and chair legs to be positioned flush with the floor. The door frames have been cut out to give depth to the panels of the cupboard door.

Yesterday's News

As the background on this picture is very faint, only the main elements have been emphasised. The ground has been raised and extra depth has been given to the cabbage patch making the picture slightly higher on the left side.

This picture, along with the others in the series (see opposite and page 75), are all mounted in the same way to reflect the colours of the period. Once framed, they will create a focal point on any wall.

Framing Your Work

If you have spent a lot of time producing a picture that you wish to keep, then you should consider having it framed.

A three-dimensional decoupage picture is obviously deeper than a single print and therefore the frame or moulding has to be deep enough to accept it – a depth of 20mm (¾in) should be sufficient.

Alternatively, a shallower moulding can have a suitable box added to the back to create additional depth. Note that the moulding should be wide enough to 'hide' the box behind it when it is mounted on a wall.

Within the frame, the picture is surrounded by mounts or mats, which are produced in numerous colours, shades and textures. The selection of colour, size and number of the mounts, in conjunction with the moulding, is very important.

Remember that you frame a picture to protect and enhance it. The choice of frame and mounts should complement the picture, so make make your selection accordingly.

As a final note, it is a mistake to select a frame to match your curtains or furniture – a picture is forever, but you might wish to redecorate! Good luck.